HUANG PO

AND THE

DIMENSIONS

OF LOVE

Crab Orchard Series in Poetry
Open Competition Award

HUANG PO AND THE DIMENSIONS OF LOVE

WALLY SWIST

CRAB ORCHARD REVIEW &
SOUTHERN ILLINOIS UNIVERSITY PRESS
Carbondale and Edwardsville

15 14 13 12   4 3 2 1

The Crab Orchard Series in Poetry is a joint publishing venture
of Southern Illinois University Press and Crab Orchard Review.
This series has been made possible by the generous support of
the Office of the President of Southern Illinois University and
the Office of the Vice Chancellor for Academic Affairs and
Provost at Southern Illinois University Carbondale.

Crab Orchard Series in Poetry Editor: Jon Tribble
Open Competition Award Judge for 2011: Yusef Komunyakaa

Library of Congress Cataloging-in-Publication Data
Swist, Wally.
Huang Po and the dimensions of love / Wally Swist.
p. cm. — (The Crab Orchard series in poetry)
ISBN-13: 978-0-8093-3099-7 (PBK. : ALK. PAPER)
ISBN-10: 0-8093-3099-7 (PBK. : ALK. PAPER)
ISBN-13: 978-0-8093-3100-0 (EBOOK)
ISBN-10: 0-8093-3100-4 (EBOOK)
I. Title.
PS3569.W58H83 2012
811'.54—dc22   2012005750

Printed on recycled paper. ♻
The paper used in this publication meets the minimum
requirements of American National Standard for Information
Sciences—Permanence of Paper for Printed Library Materials,
ANSI Z39.48-1992. ∞

For the readers of these poems

CONTENTS

ACKNOWLEDGMENTS

Grateful acknowledgment is made to the editors of the following publications in which these poems originally appeared, often in earlier versions:

2River View: "To Psyche"

Alimentum: The Literature of Food: "Cinnamon Sticks"

The Amherst Historical Society Newsletter: "The Jones Library Pine"

Angel Face: "Threshold"

Appalachia: "In the Silence," "Roaring Falls: Mid-March," "Sharp-Shinned Hawk," "Snow Geese"

Apple Valley Review: A Journal of Contemporary Literature: "The Annunciation"

Arabesques Review (Algeria): "If It Is Meant To Be"

Common Ground Review: "Breaking Open Garlic," "Coming Home," "A Deeper Quiet, Then Silence," "In the Silence" (as "Pause"), "Kingdom of Heaven"

Lalitamba: "The Locomotive"

The Larcom Review: "Just Dizzy with Love"

Many Hands: A Magazine for Holistic Health: "Among Fireflies," "The Angel," "Huang Po and the Dimensions of Love," "Hummingbird and Star," "The Locomotive," "Mount Toby, Spring Thaw," "Mystery," "Visiting Jack Gilbert at Fort Juniper," "Walking Stick"

New England Watershed Magazine: "Living in the Moment"

Osiris: "My Death" "Roaring Brook," "Starflower," "Taking It Back with Me," "The Use of Natural Objects"

Puckerbrush Review: "Accompaniment," "Almost Drowning," "The Fire," "Great Blue," "Juncos," "Listening To Rilke," "Moving the Woodpile," "Not Finding Something," "Ode to Squash Soup," "October," "Oracle," "Putting Up the Mailbox," "A Sprig of Wild Roses," "What Is Familiar," "What Remains"

Sahara: A Journal of New England Poetry: "The Annunciation," "Blue," "Grace," "Fort Juniper, Midsummer," "Kisses," "March Wind," "Mnemosyne," "Radiance," "Red-Tailed Hawk," "Rituals," "Snowdrops, Fort Juniper," "Trailing Arbutus," "Upon Request," "*Wabi* and *Sabi*," "Winter Gloves"

Sanctuary: The Massachusetts Audubon Magazine: "The Rush of the Brook Stills the Mind"

Snowy Egret: "Scrub Meadow"

"Accompaniment" originally appeared in an earlier version as a letterpress limited edition broadside issued by Adastra Press.

"Among Fireflies" was reprinted in *The 2008 Lunar Calendar* (Luna Press).

"Breaking Open Garlic," "Kingdom of Heaven," and "Mystery" were reprinted in *Arabesques Review* (Algeria).

"A Deeper Quiet, Then Silence" was reprinted in *Rosebud*.

"March Wind" was collected in *Solace in So Many Words* (Hourglass Books/ Weighed Words).

"Putting Up the Mailbox" was issued as a letterpress limited edition broadside by Timberline Press.

Some of the following poems appeared in *Mount Toby Poems,* a letterpress limited edition published by Timberline Press of Fulton, Missouri.

Acknowledgment is made to the Connecticut Commission on the Arts for an Artists Fellowship in Poetry that facilitated the writing of the initial drafts of some of these poems.

Grateful appreciation is made to the Robert Francis Trust for awarding me two back-to-back one-year residencies at Fort Juniper, the Robert Francis Homestead, in Cushman, Massachusetts, where the early drafts of some of these poems were composed and, on a rare occasion, where the poems themselves were finished.

HUANG PO

AND THE

DIMENSIONS

OF LOVE

OCTOBER

after Antonio Machado

You will want to write the word
in broad strokes on a wall,

and the voice said: *October,*
as I waved away the golden bees all summer.

Wait, the voice said, when I swept out the cabin,
and every time I scythed the land

I cleared last autumn, *October,* the voice said.
Once, I watched mating red-tailed hawks

streak and circle around the massive trunks
of the white pines, then perch on the limbs

of two saplings, *October,*
the voice said, the limbs bent down

with their weight in the heat.
When they turned their heads,

the golden pupils of their eyes widened,
and they flew up in tandem

to cut between the thick trees on the other side
of Market Hill Road, leaving

the *key-key-key-key* of their calls
whistling in me all summer.

So, when I raked the fallen leaves and pine needles,
and finally repaired the shed door

where a red squirrel gnawed through last winter,
with some scrap pine from Cowles Lumber,

I heard the voice, *October*, and thought:
What have the golden bees of summer

been doing making honey out of my old failures?
Tonight, when I stand outside,

an owl hoots and hoots; my breath steams the air,
and the first hard frost spreads its silver crystals

through the boreal forest, then begins
to shine through the moonlight in October.

MYSTERY

Somehow I could tell you entered
the cabin, and before I unlock the door,

I check for the extra key beneath
the brick at the southwest corner.

Somehow I know it has been moved—
that it is not where it was before.

I imagine I can inhale the aroma
of your skin within the sweet scent

of the pine this cabin was built with.
I know how your aura moves across

any room, trailing those blue and gold lights—
how you must have listened to the wind

singing through the remaining leaves
of the trees in the late October rain.

I know what appears to be madness
sometimes can be love, that it is

something more inconsistent,
and then even more constant, and always

more beautiful than any of that—
so that it remains a mystery

that no one else, especially
the two of us, can understand.

SNOW GEESE

Their honking and trumpeting precede them
through the canopy of leafless trees and pine branches.

We look up to see white feathers—Oh
roundness of heavy bodies exultant in air!

We watch the wedge drive over the woods,
streaming slowly, one by one—a flurry

of black wing tips that stroke against the clouds.
Before the notes of their throats fade,

we bathe in the shower of their praise—then snow
begins to drift into the silence of their passage.

A DEEPER QUIET, THEN SILENCE

Sometimes the quiet here in the cabin
is so keen that there's a ringing that comes with it—

a kind of burning away of inequities,
the way Isis placed the queen's baby daughter

into the flames, then turned her into a sparrow
that flew around the room whenever the queen entered.

The quiet and silence restorative, then I enter
the sound of the river from the bridge above it.

What is restorative is in the cleansing of that:
being filled by the movement in the rush of the water.

What is cleansing is in how the river streams
to flow beyond us, healing us with the sound of its rush,

before I walk back to the cabin,
and reenter a deeper quiet, then silence.

VISITING JACK GILBERT
AT FORT JUNIPER

He is shivering beside the hearth,
a fringed alpaca draped over his shoulders,

the shock of white hair disheveled;
his beard bearing the stubble of a few days

deep in thought of how he might outwit
Capablanca, call checkmate on his next move.

He is talking about *wabi*, the aesthetic spirit
the Japanese place in things that are worn,

or impoverished, and he recounts the beauty
and inner light of the weathered wooden

shingles of the houses in the seaside villages.
He shifts in the seat he has made of a crate

placed on end to tend the poor fire
with the iron poker, somehow the thawing

iced logs beginning to spark. He relates
how he visited a poet who played the piano,

who sang out each line to the rhythm struck
on the keys, who composed as he played

and sang as he wrote. He mentions
the man's unkempt white hair, how he just sat

at the *maestro*'s feet. On the rug in front
of the hearth, I think, *Just the way I'm sitting,*

as he bends to work the poker among
the cordwood that begins to burst into flame.

JUNCOS

I spoke with my friend earlier in the week,
who said she had seen them in her yard,

although I hadn't seen them yet in mine:
those cheery seed-eaters with small pink beaks,

sporting smart suits of charcoal-gray feathers,
whose appearance marks winter's inaugural,

no matter what the date on the calendar.
This morning, when pouring coffee

into the thermos in the galley kitchen,
I hear one *thump*, then another, against

the panes of the outer storm sash
I had put up, then cleaned to an open clarity.

Only after a second *thud* do I look out to see
the gray trail of one of their low arcs returning

to perch on one of the leafless
branches of a hickory sapling, where two

of my morning visitants look in at me—
a pair of juncos announcing their spirited arrival

by glancing off the panes of this cabin,
before they fly up, ahead of the driving snow.

THE ANNUNCIATION

after the painting by Sandro Botticelli, circa 1485

Having taken the bodily shape of a man,
Gabriel is struck by the weight
of the news he delivers upon entering

the threshold where Mary kneels,
cloistered in the room beyond;
the spoken words nearly making

the archangel stumble, his cape trailing
behind him. A gilded ray of light radiates
above his upturned wings and the sprig

of lilies he cradles in his left hand;
the transparent plane of his halo
holding a constellation of golden stars;

his right hand pulling up his gown
to brace his bowing in obeisance.
Upon hearing his greeting, Mary

is troubled, and begins to draw the folds
of her blue cloak across her breast
into converging shadow; the arc

of her halo like a divine hand placed
behind the white veil over her head.
Is this not how we respond to first hearing

any rejoicing, especially a message
that awakens in us the beginning
of understanding, of a life's path unimagined,

or if imagined, then unrealized?
How do we accept what is miraculous,
other than by looking through the portals

of the vestibule where Gabriel
is about to bend to his knees,
where the life beyond informs us

with the voice of the words we hear,
and as Mary waits for what she is to become,
we listen as the one expectant?

HUANG PO AND THE DIMENSIONS OF LOVE

Huang Po taught his students they were already
enlightened. I know of one student of Zen

who threw a translation of Huang Po
out of his apartment window, and the book,

like a block of wood, made it, on more than one
occasion, into an open trash can beside the curb.

This is not unlike the dimensions of love:
we feel the elephant ears of it, massage

the lion's paws of it, stroke the tiger's belly
of it, and are startled by the snort

steaming from the nostrils of the horse of it
that has run the field of it. We are illumined,

but we are unwilling to acknowledge its power;
so we remain unable to find what it is in ourselves

that is either *falling in love* or *agape*;
not understanding at all nor *understanding*

what is sublime. We may be able to pick through
the litter of the streets to discover a translation

of Huang Po's teaching among the trash.
We are the ones who threw it there.

We confuse seeing the wood with the true wood,
and lose each other halfway—

we see the wood of ourselves,
but miss the divine grain of the ordinary.

TO PSYCHE

What she awakens in me is that I do recognize
her face. The light in those eyes radiant
above what is breathless. Her face changes
like the moon's phases: the crescent this morning
shining through mist, Long Mountain
deep in clouds and the dawn rising.
When we know what we want, it is just like this,
this not knowing, but thinking we know;
and all of it disappearing in the light around us.

BREAKING OPEN GARLIC

I use the base of both of my palms
to press against the bottom of the bulb.

The garlic opens into cloves that splay
across the grain of the cutting board.

When I crush the cloves so I can
peel them easily, I hear her saying,

Don't wait for me in this life, each clove
an incarnation unresolved:

some in Egypt, several in Sweden,
the last in Japan, and before her voice

dissolves like a bell, I inhale the pungent
fragrance of the unforgettable.

WHAT REMAINS

He is surprised every time he notices
he leans one of his elbows on the dining room table

with his raised hand slightly tilted back,
fingers curled, the thumb resting over them—

in which she displays her demure elegance with ease;
or when she tells him that

driving to work in the morning, when she makes
a sighting, she says *Hawk*, just the way he does.

SHARP-SHINNED HAWK

An explosion of cardinals, juncos, and black-capped
chickadees out of the nimbus

of the sugar maple's crown leaves the branches,
in one electric instant, clattering.

The sharp-shinned hawk zeros in
to settle on its target perch;

its talons curl to grip the bark.
It rides up and down: the dark flight feathers

and the under-white of its tail suggest an arrow
quivering in its mark. Still, the disappointment

of the hunt reveals itself in the unnerving, slight
twitches of tail feathers, the slow

rotation of its head from side to side.
Then it stretches out of its fierce, hunched posture,

flies up, veering out of the maple, off
on a sharp angle toward the back pasture.

Just when it begins to rise in the wind, it disappears
on the deception of exquisite bones.

SNOWDROPS, FORT JUNIPER

for Robert Francis

They bloom through each blanket
of March snow, and I am unable

to believe they are blossoming
after my winter of solitude.

When the snow melts, I can't help
but see them: these augurs of spring

that offer the fragrance
of the wind that blows over new snow,

the three white, waxy petals
on their small tubular stems

nodding among their speared leaves.
When I walk around to the west side

of the cabin, I hear Robert's voice:
Go and see the snowdrops,

always seeing more of them, and how
they spread out, not having seen them

after twenty years, but now
seeing them again for the first time.

THE LOCOMOTIVE

She asks me if I will remember our passion.
Seated beside a window in a Pullman,

passing through the countryside in spring,
a signpost of a village flashes before our eyes.

There is a red barn beside the station, a pond
reflecting sky, and pink blossoms falling above

the white chickens. Traveling in the locomotive
of the heart, we must always try to appraise

what we can keep and how much
of the extraordinary we must learn to let go of,

how much of us, *as limitless as passion can be,*
will remain; how we may be able

to break past that to find ourselves
more aware of a radiance than a blinding light,

destined, as we are, to arrive
somewhere between moving and standing still.

FORT JUNIPER, MIDSUMMER

The sprinkling of sap pelts the understory
of hickory and maple leaves

from the towering branches of white pine.
Amber rain falls through the simmer of wind

from the canopy in the sunlight.
I sweat to the swing of each

sweep of the blade that scythes
the overgrowth around the cabin.

When I stop to rest, and lean on the handle,
curved like an egret's neck,

I inhale the sweetness of the fragrance
released by my strides through the swale,

and listen to the lucid notes
of a warbler's song honey the air.

THRESHOLD

When he remembers the beginning, he looks
out the front windows of the cabin to the hills
and the colors of autumn this afternoon
in the sunlight, and thinks of her warmth,
her laughter. He remembers what was
beyond her smile, and thinking this
is all that matters: that continuum, that going
beyond they both enter, and a door
opens across another threshold,
where there is nothing but light, pure light.

UPON REQUEST

On Lincoln Street in Hartford, I listened
to a Mr. Softee's ice cream truck

endlessly circle the streets to replay
the hurdy-gurdy of its jingle

through nearly every season for three years.
Either too early in the morning or too late

at night, some people chose
to use their car horn instead of a doorbell.

Sometimes, I was awakened
to gunshots fired at four AM.

Here, in this cabin in Cushman, I listen
to the silence after the crickets

have stopped answering the cicadas.
I see the leaves of the sugar maple brighten

to a deeper orange, hay-scented fern begin
to bronze in the sun, and inhale a fragrance

of cinnamon, the scent of their giving up
their lushness for something other.

RITUALS

At twilight, I walk the land I cleared
of brier, pigweed, and nettle,

turn to look through the kitchen
window on the side of the cabin,

know the warmth there inside
by the lights I turned on.

There are mornings I watch dawn
fill the grove of pine and hickory,

see stars in the cup of the dipper
through treetops, hear an owl hoot,

as it changes its perch from one limb
to another in the woods

on the ridge across Market Hill Road.
But at twilight I find stillness in the falling

of pine needles, how they spread out
over open ground, and it is in stillness,

I remember how I brush back her hair,
take her face in my hands, so I can see

what shines there, the way sudden wind
lifts branches to allow a slant of light

to make yellow hickory leaves more yellow
and its green leaves more green.

GRACE

Driving country roads this Sunday
in November, I notice a marsh hawk

perched above the berm of the shoulder,
disguised in its beige and gray feathers

on a branch of a leafless maple.
I see a large patch of silver dollars

refracting the slant of the sun;
the remaining leaves of prairie willows,

their silver undersides upturned in the wind;
coils of bittersweet bursting with

split orange and yellow berries among
branches of beech saplings, whose leaves

are various tones of russet and rust.
When I stop by the Mill River, a voice

rings inside me: *It is always
a good time to pray*, and I do so for us both,

beside the swimming hole we cooled off in
last summer. When I return to

the quiet of this cabin, I could choose
to fly into one project after another,

but I know what I need is to slow down,
to not only listen to my own voice,

but to go deeply enough within myself
to hear yours, and I find your face

just under the surface of mine, this light
beneath my skin that will not die.

NOT FINDING SOMETHING

I have always wanted to find a match
for her silver earring, whose shape is a whorl

of a leaf, that just fits the form of the lobe
of her ear, although she lost it years before

we ever met, as if in doing so I could resolve
the negotiation of our renewal of bliss.

I know I may never find a match for it
when I step out tonight in November rain

to shine the flashlight on the old raccoon
in his wizened fur, who doesn't lift

the black mask of his head,
how he muddles about in the fallen leaves.

WINTER GLOVES

Snow falls this afternoon, sleet ticks
against the tin stovepipe on the roof.

When I step outside to walk into the white
of its falling, I look up at the tall pine tops,

then over to the chimney of this cabin,
think how transitory the snow, how mortar

and brick have outlasted storm and ice.
I see how the pines remain true

to themselves, their trunks straight,
the tops shape-shifted by wind.

What is true is somewhere between
what I believe and what I say,

what she tells me and how she means it—
and we do not reach the middle path:

her sash tied across her waist,
my robe open for her.

When I awaken this morning,
after hard frost, I pull on the winter gloves

she gave me last Christmas
that hold a strand of her long white hair.

TRAILING ARBUTUS

I look for you intently, on my knees, among
drifted leaf litter near mountain summits, to find

your small, almost translucent, white petals,
blushing pink, barely open. Once, only

too common, you were sold on street corners
in Boston in the 1890s. Your shy flowers

are hidden beneath your rough, oval evergreen
leaves that too soon turn brown, but to have

inhaled your redolence is to know the sweet
excess of more than enough, why you are

also known as *the poet's flower.*
Little flower of irony, impatient to bloom

even before the last patches of snow begin
to melt, you are too quick to vanish.

ACCOMPANIMENT

Not unlike the yellow birch leaf
we saw suspended above the edge

of the trail by a thread of a spider's web
in autumn rain on Mount Toby, what remains

of us in the warmth of spring sunlight
in a meadow in Conway is still held

in abeyance above bedstraw and meadow grass.
I have thought of you often this morning.

You don't know this. And you don't need me
to tell you, but I need you to know that

you accompany me into the world
like a rose opening.

RED-TAILED HAWK

Late autumn, standing on the fire tower
on top of Mount Toby, to hear

its wings snap like a heavy sheet
in the wind, then watch it glide

on a thermal, but to have the chance
to turn to look around,

and see the curve of its beak, the flash
of its tail, and for it to vanish

before I am fully aware, is in keeping
with you to be free to choose.

The distance between us
speaks for itself, and I want you

to know what you need,
out of who you are,

the way a red-tailed hawk
crosses the ridges of this valley.

THE INSPIRED LIFE

Angels speak homeopathy fluently.

CAROLINE MYSS

The fingers of my hands find
a way to her the other evening,

working out the kink in the right side
of her neck, and when the muscles

finally relax, she releases
one audible sigh, *Oh*.

Blue morning glories spiral above
white trillium, their petals opened

beneath their diamond-shaped leaves.
The wood pewee calls out above us

among the trellises in the garden,
and the one this morning answers

from her perch over the trail above me;
the pattern of a shepherd's crook

uncurling in every fiddlehead
that rises through the ground.

A SPRIG OF WILD ROSES

a Ghazal in Memory of Agha Shahid Ali

Wind sweeps through the pin oaks at the summit,
falling acorns punctuate each wave at the summit.

A cloud of topsoil dissolves above a field
beyond the trees, when I just look out at the summit.

Before blowing cumulus darkens them, I see
sunlight strike ripples in the river below at the summit.

On Mount Toby, Japanese knotweed rustles in the shade:
a dry brush painting, in green ink, at the summit.

My inner voice, attentive caretaker,
reasons with me, and says out loud, *Look!*, at the summit.

Ripened raspberries redden a thicket on the trail.
Wind tugs at wild roses in my backpack at the summit.

The sprig I placed in the netting: each petal fragrant,
unfurls like a flag of my desire at the summit.

TAKING IT BACK WITH ME

I take the bracing cold down with me
from the fire tower at Mount Toby's summit.

I take the quality of the light with me—
its gold polish and September clarity;

the flash of those steel girders,
the breadth of the view: Monadnock's

granite dome just a touch north-northeast,
Greylock's prominence due west,

Snow's jagged peak at eleven o'clock.
I take the sound of the wind with me,

the invisible surf spreading
through treetops across this valley.

I stand on the wooden platform
of the top tier, my hands holding

onto a bend in the metal guardrail,
the Connecticut River flowing below,

swollen after days of rain, and before
taking it back with me, I watch

that one red oak leaf above the tree line,
suspended and spinning in the cross drafts.

ROARING BROOK

The running luminescence
    of the sluice unwinding
        down the pudding-stone slope,

laced with white foam,
    creating one *s* after another;
        the word *silver* nearly audible

in the sound of its rush;
    the splash and churn
        at each bend and cascade.

Slanted beams of sunlight
    filling its effervescence and every pool;
        the effluence pouring

out of the culvert;
    the sound of the flow of what is infinite,
        framed in the moment,

or of say, just being able
    to glance at all that is written
        on the long wall of the *akasha*.

The sounds of the water
    falling down the mountain,
        sliding from consonance

to assonance so many times
    they entwine to become the spool
        of a spoken word, voice itself, fluidity.

LIVING IN THE MOMENT

It is in knowing which particular
mineral is the one to take home
to mark this day's hike up the mountain

that might grace the *kata*
on the mantel of the fireplace
or one of the cabin's pine windowsills.

It is in choosing among the gleam
of quartz and the glistening of mica
as to what may remind you of the wind

in your ears at the summit.
It is in sensing a presence
in the clearing at dusk before

the snort of the startled doe's breath
clouds beneath the gibbous moon,
and its hooves clatter over the stones.

MOUNT TOBY, SPRING THAW

The trickle of melting ice
catches in the basin beneath the culvert,
flows ledge to ledge, then descends

the stony bed worn between the banks
of the gorge. Runoff flashes
along the shoot of the frozen falls—

the thaw of the brook pausing
across a long table of snow-encrusted rock
before it tumbles over the rim of another.

The sluice slides down the doglegs
of ice, spills ribbons of water that plunge
through the beams of sunlight illuminating

each pool, and where, mid-mountain,
I stop to watch the rippling
water shadows silver the mossy cliffs.

SCRUB MEADOW

At the foot of Mount Toby, on a rise above Cranberry Pond,
I wade through clusters of St.-John's-wort's yellow corollas.

A dragonfly bends back a bristly stem of bottlebrush grass.
The rayed flowers of yarrow offer a sweet aroma

when rubbed between fingers into the palm.
I brush tall blooms of mullein that open out a softness

from their basal leaves. Candles of their petals burn bright
in the hot July sun. I watch grasshoppers vault

pearly stands of sweet white clover. I find the meadow within,
waist-deep in fleabane, turning the wind lavender.

ROARING FALLS: MID-MARCH

The stream rushes in sunlight
and a smell of decay rises through mist

that blows across drifted banks of snow.
Hiking the mountain to the falls, I pause,

listen to water flowing over stones.
A white birch trunk revolves in the rhythm

of an eddy in the basin below, the roar
of plunging water patterned within

ripples of the pool, within rings
of the tree itself; and here it's refoliated—

the spray of the falls, melting, refreezing—
along its branches, the clear icy leaves.

MY DEATH

The pigeons fly up past windowpanes
to the rooftops, then beyond

the rooftops. Pigeons fly up, not doves.
The dirge of traffic grinds to a stop.

Someone tries to rub a cinder from an eye,
and so much sunlight streaks

the brownstones a comforting rust.
This is it, the perpetuity of it all,

as I look up at the sheer face
of these cliffs, suddenly bright with patches

of moss and wild with the shaggy white
petals of wood asters.

What I have become is this
emptiness that rests within the cusp

of an open semicircle
embraced by fronds of maidenhair.

THE RUSH OF THE BROOK
STILLS THE MIND

The trail flashes
    with sluices of snowmelt.
        Silver-green undersides

of hemlock lift in the wind.
    A warbler's electric call
        climbs all the way

up the mountain slope.
    That hidden waterfall
        we promised to see

this spring unrolls bolt after bolt
    of runoff that splashes
        veils of watery lace

over stones. The canopy
    creaks with pine siskins.
        Mist rises above snow.

The aloneness almost too much
    for one man. The surge
        of the brook crashes

around boulders; a sinkhole
    swirls and dips. Ripples
        cascade in a basin

under deadfall to plunge
    into a froth of torrent.
        A nuthatch debugs

a fallen branch that rocks
in the current; and a mayfly
is blown above the spray.

STARFLOWER

Star of the upland woodlands,
seven-petaled, not unlike

the Pleiades' seven sisters,
you speckle the new green

of the undergrowth beside
the loose talus of the trail

like flecks of sea foam amid
a bed of browned pine needles.

Wherever you bloom, starflower,
your china white blazes, fixed

like a pattern of starlight,
your petals a constellation

set among the shade spread along
the mountain path every May.

I see you everywhere
since now I know your name.

JUST DIZZY WITH LOVE

On the shore of Cranberry Pond,
    a mud dauber wasp rises
        and falls, then begins

to knead the gleaming gray mud.
    He labors like an instrument,
        a barometer of buzz,

who performs an earthy bebop,
    just like a saxophone.
        He intently repeats

an incantation, the same
    insect scales. His solo
        drones on and on

for his queen, whose
    dark chitinous body
        he conjures, his blind

allegiance dizzy
    with love. Dip, then let
        the notes fly formidably

around the tossing
    grasses, this reedy pond.
        Sting the air with sound.

LISTENING TO RILKE

He says that my mother's death
spreads out in both directions: to a point

that was and a point that will be.
I am fifty, he says, but

the eight-year-old in me stands
behind me in the shadow I cast

like a son who defers to his father.
He tells me he has begun

to make me believe that my actions
resemble those of a man who has

broken through something inside of himself.
His is the voice inside me that asks:

How aware are you? and says
There is no time, when I stand

in patches of sunlight that shine
through the forest canopy where

I listen to the rush of the brook
fall down the mountain slope,

and watch wave after wave of wind
break in the trees, whose sound

cleanses me like nothing else.
Rainer, my friend, one of *my* angels,

how ardently I listen to you,
as on the darkest of nights

when I walk for hours among
the snowy pages of your poems,

whose words glow like ingots
in the moonlight. In a dream,

when you appear to me, I have
needed to shield my eyes from

the cloud of light that surrounds you.
When I listen to the panther

you saw in the Jardin des Plantes
pace in its cage, sometimes, I too,

can feel my hands move beneath me,
as they write. How much I know

how difficult it is to revise
my life. What it is to remember,

at twenty, after first discovering
your poems, how I would stand out on

the library steps at dusk, one after another
for many dusks, and choose a star

burning above a dark doorway, filled
with awe of what it is *to be a beginner*

and *always having to begin.*
Sometimes when I am listening to you,

I become happy enough to stop to look up
on the mountain trail to identify

the trees by the shape of their leaves:
tulip, pignut hickory, white oak, sassafras,

and striped maple, then be able,
from a far-ranging cliff, to inhale

the fragrance of the hayed fields
below, the sweetness rising.

KISSES

Is the reason why I climb the trail up
the mountain to be reminded of her body,

to breathe in the scent of cinnamon
released in one shaft of sun after another

from the ferns that lie beyond?
When I am reminded of the fragrance

of her body, why do I imagine a trail
of smoke, as from an offering of incense,

taper upward, before it disappears
into the light? And why is it

after I place kisses over her body,
I inhale the redolence of ferns

on the mountain trail before
we leave the bed to rise in the morning?

WALKING STICK

Take all away from me, but leave me Ecstasy.

EMILY DICKINSON

If you make a gift of your walking stick —
     make it a thick pine branch,
          stripped of the bark—

the one that has accompanied you
     on many hikes. Let it be
          the one that has secured

your steps on Toby, Grace,
     and Lafayette. Brush the wood
          with layers of polyurethane,

cincture the top with a sash
     of wound leather strips,
          tied in a bow knot;

then insert hawk feathers
     to billow above the woven cords.
          En prana it

to guide her on a trail in the wild.
     By your making it a gift, *bless her*
          as she walks wherever she walks,

so that she may remember:
     she is one with everything—
          that she is safe whenever she walks.

It is imperfectly fashioned,
     unlike your *Ecstasy*, but it is
          designed to remind her of that.

HUMMINGBIRD AND STAR

Whether we sit hip to hip on a boulder
in the middle of Roaring Brook—

our feet cooling in the rush;
or whether we picnic in a hayed meadow

looking up at summer sky.
That simplicity is what we

try to live out of. Promise me
you will remember the hummingbird

pollinating those blue
irises purpling the banks of the reservoir—

what we find in each other's face
that radiates like the light of a star.

AMONG FIREFLIES

Their blinking lights surround me.
I enter each wave of birch and beech

in the green darkness, and crest
through needles of hemlocks—

a nebula expands around me.
I cup some in my hands, open

my palm's pink cave to see how
they flicker there. I lift them up

to let each go beneath the treetops,
and the moon begins to rise.

ODE TO SQUASH SOUP

I strip the skin
        from the curves
                of butternut squash

with a paring knife;
        with the butcher knife,
                slice them in half;

take a soupspoon,
        remove the pulp and seeds;
                halve them again,

then halve the cubes,
        and set them aside.
                I peel potatoes,

scrub carrots, then dice them.
        I crush a bulb of garlic
                with the back of my hand,

and supply it
        to the chicken stock
                I pour into the pot;

immerse the vegetables;
        let them simmer.
                The windows mist,

the broth thickens.
        I add bay leaves;
                white pepper; rosemary,

for earthy fragrance;
      a touch of dry vermouth.
            I puree this in the blender,

then grate *Parmesan*
      for flavor. I ladle
            myself a bowl,

and before I dip my spoon,
      I taste the soup's sweetness
            in the steam rising.

THE ANGEL

thinks I need to be awakened
to hear the freight at three AM

and its lumbering over the tracks
a half a mile down Market Hill Road

in Cushman's center—a twinkling
of stars across the bowl of the sky.

The angel's hair streams, as she stands
on a flatbed, the countryside of rime

and ice spread beyond the stiff wings
that rise above her shoulders

and the fluttering of her gown before
the leaden drumming of the freight

drones to a pause in the train's passing.
Light emerges from the angel's face

like the moon rising above the pines,
the index finger of one hand pointing

from where she now leans over
the caboose's railing, bitter wind

swirling beneath the eaves, the spangled
design of icicles and frost flowers

embroidered across her bodice, the hem
of her skirt, and the edges of her sleeves.

The feathery rasp of the angel's voice
steams in a cloud: *Divine each day,*

choose to write words that praise,
that open out of the center of everything.

THE FIRE

He gathers cordwood into his arms,
lays each piece on the grates

in the hearth, two across and two over;
sets balled newsprint with a match,

and the wood and paper blaze up
in a *whoosh* of brightness.

He first watches the blue flames,
then the white, those lights they see

when they are together,
the incandescent tongues that burst

above his head when he speaks to her
about what they share is sacred.

He considers what light and warmth are,
that the glow of the fire doesn't compare

to what shines in her face, that rose
beneath the surface of her skin.

When he banks up burning embers
with the long-handled shovel, then uses

the iron tongs to gather the fallen
ingots of wood back onto the grates,

he leans into the fire, and hears her voice
when he was above her, praying for her

silently, with her hands on his back,
how she told him, *I can feel the heat.*

MARCH WIND

It blows loose brush and leaves into the air
across the opening of the field. Walk into it

and it tugs at your jacket, brushes back your hair.
It reawakens you to the persistent cold of winter,

despite your seeing spring in shoals of snowdrops
breaking through a crust of late snow.

It assuages you by its bitterness,
knifes through your layers: what your lover said,

then what she did, clarifies your aloneness.
It reminds you that the future is incalculable.

It begins to make you ready
to accept what is revealed in what is difficult.

It howls every time
it cuts loose the sorrow that weighs down the past.

BLUE

In the photograph, the dress
my mother is wearing is periwinkle blue,

the pumps she has slipped into
a powder blue. The boutonniere

pinned to one of the lapels
of my father's beige suit is slate blue.

The steadfast eyes of my mother and father
are a discernible blue.

They stand in front of my father's Woody
on their wedding day.

The polished wood on its sides
contrasts the shades of blue

in the browned photograph.
The Woody's chrome and hubcaps sparkle.

Its burgundy hood and fenders shine.
Even the silver clouds suspended

in the gunmetal sky augur the intimations
of a color as blue as cerulean.

Neither one dreamed she would collapse,
or he would be consumed by drifting

deeper into the emptiness of a smoky blue haze.
The thought never occurred to them

my father would bury my mother,
and that he would not remember her

ever wearing that brocaded dress
and blue satin shoes.

ORACLE

Grandmother's doily-covered upholstery
and embroidered couch and pillow coverlets glimmered

in the parlor with the onset of my mother's headaches
and the closing of the blinds to the stereoscopic light

of migraines the year before the cerebral hemorrhage.
I watched my mother sleep, engaged

in such single-minded protection I dozed myself,
until the magic of *Charlie Chan and His Favorite Sons*

began on television at four o'clock.
My father arrived from the plant

where he spent eight hours in oil up to his armpits,
washing machine parts for Pratt & Whitney,

that led to his frustration, due to his broken
English and his outbursts in Polish,

kicking the dog at the threshold.
One afternoon after her nap, my mother offered

from the armchair, *If I die first, you will have trouble*
with your father. You will have a difficult time

keeping a job. She paused into the dead zone
of the parlor's darkness, a gravity holding the dust motes

in abeyance: *You will never find anyone to love;*
my mother's gift to me, the honey of my own failures.

THE USE OF NATURAL OBJECTS

For a year after my mother died,
my father wore a black armband,

and the cold surrounded us.
I was unable to remember the last time

I saw her, when she walked me
to school on the first day of third grade.

Afterwards, she climbed the several
sets of concrete steps up the steep

slope to the apartment, then scaled
the three flights of stairs to where

she collapsed on the floor.
The year my mother died, my father

assisted me with a school project
that required the use of natural objects.

We constructed an Eskimo village
out of eggshells and cotton, a diorama

of igloos in a shoe box, my father's
black armband riding his biceps,

as we worked our gloveless
fingers in the cold surrounding us.

IF IT IS MEANT TO BE

That first Sunday in Whately, a cabbage white floats
beyond us, as if our energy together is the wind itself.

We talk about learning how to play "Silver Bells"
on the piano, so we can sing it at Christmas.

When you ask, *What is your favorite piece?*, both
of us choose the pleasing simplicity of the celadon

Chinese bowl; the Turkish candelabra, ornamented
with gilt-leaved loops around each candlestick

that open with the signature of infinity; the three
duodecimal volumes bound in the sensuality

of 15th-century Italian vellum. We walk in our own
sweet music, that easy wind that makes the pleats

of your skirt swirl, causes the creases of my slacks
to ripple. You see me in the shells in the bell jar

on the ledge of your office window.
When Rilke speaks about his hands, as he writes,

having a life of their own, you go on beyond me
somewhere, and I know I am a happy part of you.

KINGDOM OF HEAVEN

The father's kingdom is spread out upon the earth
and people do not see it.

THE GOSPEL OF THOMAS

After judging each wreath
hung on every door on Beacon Hill

on a scale of one to five stars,
we sit facing each other Christmas evening

in the bedroom in your Aunt Striddie's
Empire chairs. Streetlights illumine

the blizzard's gusts that shine
over the snow angels we made—

the candles blown out in the igloo
of snowballs we built to house them in.

You ask me: *How does this begin?*
and *Why don't other people want this?*

Beneath the lamplight, I draw breath,
the freckles on your Scandinavian face

only even more abundant on the long
fingers of your elegant hands. I say:

It starts with the meeting of our eyes,
and *Too often it is what people do not see.*

RADIANCE

Over your gray and white oval marble-top kitchen table,
the meeting of our eyes makes the room grow brighter.
Our faces, layer after layer, become so vibrant

the light appears to crest in waves.
We have become changed by it, nothing can be
the same after it. When I bend down to touch

the shape of deer tracks in the damp sand, it is in
the same way I place my fingers over your body.
When I stand beside a freshet in a meadow

the sun catches the rings of the water's long ripples
in the wind, that is the same glimmer we hold
when our eyes meet in the kitchen over

your gray and white oval marble-top table.
Every day for the rest of my life, yours is the face
I want to see when I awake in the morning.

MNEMOSYNE

They are happy, they are just beginning. They sit and talk
about their need for simplicity, and the tension between them

grows, the way iron filaments are drawn by a magnet.
Before he kisses her, he notices the curves of her breasts

beneath the black crinoline dress; then how everything
ceases except the touch of what is sensual.

He looks at her face in the sun, the small blue veins that etch
her closed eyelids, after he opens his, the beads of sweat above

her lips. This is the beginning of their learning what is sublime:
how they stand on East Beach, and look over at Block Island;

how they watch the green sea spread out at low tide,
the surf entreating them with the *adagio*

of what is susurrant; how they hold each other against the wind
that doesn't appear to ripple the water.

WHAT IS FAMILIAR

is how I massage those ropes
of tightened muscles across

your shoulders and upper back,
placing my hands beneath the top

of your blouse, while I stand
behind you beside the kitchen sink,

so I may be able to work
what is tender loose.

I read your skin as I would a map,
my fingers adept at locating the pain

there with the pressure of my touch.
You ask me, *Do you hear it pop?*

and then I feel your release.
What is familiar are the kisses

I place on your bare shoulders,
grateful for the gift

of those moments, before we spend
the remainder of the afternoon

bundling magazines with string
for the Salvation Army,

you placing your index finger
on each knot I am about to tie.

GREAT BLUE

When the great blue heron appears
    through the leaves of the trees lining
        the banks of the Farmington River,

I think of all that is marginal
    in this life compared to those
        slow, powerful wings, rowing the air

above the river's heart.
    The plumed head looks to the left,
        then to the right, as it cranes to peer

into the water of the river's
    swift current, cresting its banks,
        flowing with the rush of the insistent

June rain. And I think of you,
    and wish you had been beside me
        to see the great bird, that sacred vision,

rowing the air, and searching
    the heart of the river. So, I think, is
        this why I am alive, that being with you

is like stepping into the sunlight
    after days of rain, and to know that
        you are opening in ways you have never

opened before? I think,
    as the great blue heron flies
        out of sight, that I row the air above

the river of your heart, neither of us
being able to comprehend those powerful
wings, unable to gauge that the vision

of the epiphanal would be a reason
anyone standing on the banks would
want to break into song, and might

even propel the heron further into
following the strong current of you,
surging past the low-hung tendriled leaves.

WABI AND SABI

We rub our hands over the bench along the trail
to feel what weather has worn,

how storms have polished the pine wood—
she flows inside of me like a spring.

Other times, she becomes the wind
in the trees, the trailing voices of geese.

On those mornings, I watch the light
rise in her to rekindle her face—

the way she looked, that Sunday, across
the wildflower meadow at Northwest Park:

Deptford pink, black-eyed Susan,
the open white parasols of Queen Anne's lace.

I know when I become as obdurate as stone,
the Christ in me breaks the stone in two,

and I become a fountain
pouring out of the cleaved rock.

THE JONES LIBRARY PINE

Most obvious are the uppermost
branches bundled with cones,

three thick trunks growing halfway
up the girth of the rooted one,

the trailing top, splayed and bending,
its evergreen prayer flags unfurled.

How it exemplifies what quiet is,
having to do with the weight

its heavy branches bear
with the spirit of such *lightness*.

The pine's presence reminds us
just to be, and although you are not

with me, I find you in the immeasurable
sifting of its branches, whose resinous

fragrance thickens at the slightest
stir of the summer wind.

ALMOST DROWNING

I want to enter the shallow end of the pond,
but you choose where it is deeper,

by the control pump on the other side.
We swim next to each other;

your overhand propels your lithe body
beyond me. My sidestroke is not as strong.

I know I won't make it. I turn around,
and you follow me back, swim beside me.

My heart pounds in my head,
breath in hard quick spurts. I begin to sink.

Don't give up. Keep going. Put your feet down.
I pull myself up to the patch of sand,

numb, beside the pump. You ask me
if I were frightened just then in the water,

you ask me what I am thinking,
the needles and leaves of the firs and sycamores

backlit in their own shadows through the dusk,
making them appear more real than real.

I tell you I did not want to finish my life
at the bottom of this pond in Conway,

and before I take your hands in mine,
early stars beginning to appear in the water,

I try to understand, when halfway to the float,
you tell me you cannot save me from drowning.

MOVING THE WOODPILE

I am rinsed in quiet living here in this cabin in the woods,
and move the woodpile this September afternoon to make room

for a clothesline between white pine and sugar maple.
Clearing the skids of wood, I discover a white-footed mouse,

who blinks, then bounds off through years of fallen leaves;
a black salamander who wriggles deeper into bark mulch;

wolf spiders who display, if not demand, their presence;
stinkbugs who drive themselves in circles like bumper cars;

and a leopard frog who jumps, then leaps, disturbing
a swath of snakeskin *rubbed off against the bark.*

I restack the wood on the skids, then chink in the splits.
When the sky clouds over, and my sweat beads on the wood,

it is filigreed with the gills of beige and white mushrooms.
After I rake that spot of chipped bark and slivers,

sunlight bolts between the leaves, and shines on cleared earth,
then lights on the newly stacked wood.

IN THE SILENCE

The ruby-red cluster of false Solomon's seal
berries stud their dangling mustard-yellow leaves.

After its shadow crosses mine,
a marsh hawk perches high on a pine limb

the guttural clicks of its call repeat,
the glint of eyes backlit against the sunset.

I listen to the crickets answer each other
all night, savor the ringing of their sprockets.

In early September cold, their voices pause,
then cease after the first hard frost.

COMING HOME

Even the kingfisher recognizes him,
although too many years have left

both of them older now.
She calls once, twice, then again:

to give him the opportunity
to spot her perching on one

of the limbs of the budding maple.
Then she flies up, leaving him

alone with the brook. A feather
bristles across the ripples of a pool.

So much forgotten, he thinks,
standing on the wooden footbridge:

how that feels like snow,
how the snow feels like heartache,

how he knows that what is difficult
is trying to live in the world.

CINNAMON STICKS

You asked me years ago, *Tell me how you know when to use them?*
I do not remember what I answered you then, but it is in their aromatic

sweetness and their pungence that they can achieve piquancy in a dish.
It can be in a simple curry, or in a *Bolognese.* Stir the cinnamon sticks

in with extra-virgin olive oil in a pan over the flame, several dashes
of coriander, cumin, garam masala, a whole bulb of crushed garlic,

diced sweet Mayan onion, chopped Holland and green bell peppers.
Then add crushed tomatoes, tomato paste, a pound of uncooked ground
beef—

the sliced zucchini goes in last—*and love, yes, an ingredient of love,*
over low heat for an hour, although it is the last component in the concoction

that neither one of us will ever forget. Seeing you standing at the crosswalk
the other day, as I did just happen to drive past, when we both waved

and smiled, made me think of your asking me about cinnamon sticks,
and how I can finally offer you an answer specific enough,

in that I use them the same way I would massage those knots loose
in the muscles of your back, then place kisses on each of your bare shoulders.

It occurred to me that I use cinnamon sticks just that way,
although I did think about another question you would ask me,

which was, *I want to know what those lights are*
when I look at you; what are those lights, and where do they come from?

After all these years of our being separate from one another,
but together being able to enter ever further into the light of what is beatific,

that shines from each of our faces, it appears through this
radiance we have become aware of that question having answered itself.

PUTTING UP THE MAILBOX

I pull up the twisted jack pine post
with gloved hands, surprised to find

I need to jerk the cinderblock
it is attached to out of the ground,

where it leaned on one side for years.
I mallet the new metal base two feet deep

with the back-edge of an axe.
The echo of my pounding on the target

2 by 4 in the center ricochets through
the woods on either side of the road.

Ravens lift above the trees to begin
their *wonk-wonk*, and with each swing

I am jolted into a joy of hammering.
After I snap down the metal locks

at the base with the strokes of a hammer,
I place the four-foot-tall milled pine post

into it, then center the white pine platform
on top, drive in wood screws to secure

the new box on both sides and in back,
then bank the base with the stones

I unearthed, and fill in the old spot with dirt.
I walk around it, to admire its height,

its straightness, its square to the road.
Now when I check the mail, I open the lid,

knowing I erected what is durable,
and raised what is reliable in myself.

NOTES

"October"

The poem alludes to "And the golden bees / were making white combs / and sweet honey / from my old failures" from "Last Night, as I Was Sleeping" by Antonio Machado. *The Winged Energy of Delight: Selected Translations* by Robert Bly (New York: HarperCollins, 2004), pages 65–66.

"Visiting Jack Gilbert at Fort Juniper," "Snowdrops, Fort Juniper," and "Fort Juniper, Midsummer"

Fort Juniper is the homestead of the late poet and writer Robert Francis (August 12, 1902, Upland, Pennsylvania–July 13, 1987, Northampton, Massachusetts), whom Robert Frost dubbed "the best unknown American poet." The cottage was built by Francis in 1940, and he lived there the rest of his life. Since the poet's passing, the homestead has been offered as a writing residency, in conjunction with the wishes the poet expressed in his will, and is overseen through the aegis of the trustees of the Robert Francis Trust.

"Visiting Jack Gilbert at Fort Juniper"

The word *wabi* may be defined as a Japanese aesthetic that honors cultivated simplicity and poverty.

"Huang Po and the Dimensions of Love"

Huang Po (also spelled Huang-po and Huángbò), whose birth date is unknown, died circa 850. Very little is known about his life for certain. There is no biographical information in the *Ch'uan-hsin Fa-yao* (Essentials of Mind Transmission) and the *Wan-ling Lu* (Record of Wan-ling), his collections of sayings and sermons. However, records indicate Huang Po was extraordinarily tall.

Beginning his monastic life on Mt. Huang Po in Fuzhou (Fu-chien) province, Huang Po received the Buddhist name Hsi-yun. Huang Po's main teacher was Baizhang Huaihai, another Mazu student, and it was from Baizhang that Huang Po received Dharma transmission. According to the commentary by Yuanwu Kequin in *The Blue Cliff Record*, when Baizhang first met Huang Po, he exclaimed, "Magnificent! Imposing! Where have you come from?" Huang Po replied, "Magnificent and imposing, I've come from the mountains."

"Trailing Arbutus"

In this poem, *the poet's flower* refers to an article, published in *West Virginia Wildlife Magazine* and written by Emily Grafton, a seasonal wildlife biologist stationed in Elkins, West Virginia, that reads in part, "Trailing arbutus was heavily collected from the wild by street vendors in 19th century New England. The 'hawkers' would fill their carts with the evergreen plants winter through spring and walk the streets of Boston yelling 'Mayflowers for sale.' This name came from the legend told by poets like Whittier and folklorists that blossoms of trailing arbutus greeted the colonists who landed at Plymouth Rock."

"Accompaniment" and "Walking Stick"
Mount Toby is located in the towns of Sunderland and Leverett, Massachusetts, and, at 1,269 feet (387 m), is the highest summit of a sprawling collection of mostly wooded hills and knolls that rise from a distinct plateau-like upland, just east of the Connecticut River. Mount Toby is notable for its waterfalls and glacial kettle ponds, especially Cranberry Pond. Although the summit is wooded, there is a fire tower, open to the public, which provides a 360-degree view of Amherst and the Holyoke Range to the south; the Connecticut River, Mount Sugarloaf, and Mount Greylock to the west; Mount Snow and Mount Monadnock to the north; and the nearby Peace Pagoda in Leverett to the east.

"The Inspired Life"
"Angels speak homeopathy fluently" is a quote from the audiobook *Spiritual Power, Spiritual Practice: Energy Evaluation Meditations for Morning and Evening* by Caroline Myss (Boulder, CO: Sounds True Audio, 2000).

"A Sprig of Wild Roses"
The dedication is to Agha Shahid Ali (February 4, 1949, New Delhi, India—December 8, 2001, Amherst, Massachusetts), a Kashmiri American poet. His poetry collections include *A Walk through the Yellow Pages*, *The Half-Inch Himalayas*, *A Nostalgist's Map of America*, *The Country without a Post Office*, and *Rooms Are Never Finished* (finalist for the National Book Award, 2001). His last book is *Call Me Ishmael Tonight*, a collection of English ghazals.

"Living in the Moment"
The word *kata* refers to the traditional white offering scarf of Tibetan origin. The *kata* is an auspicious symbol and indicates the good intentions of the person offering it. *Katas* are offered to religious images, such as statues of the Buddha.

"Walking Stick"
"Take all away from me, but leave me Ecstasy" (1885) by Emily Dickinson, *The Poems of Emily Dickinson: Reading Edition*, edited by R. W. Franklin (Cambridge: Harvard University Press, 2003), poem 1671, page 604. There are other variants.

The phrase *en prana*, whose origin is Sanskrit, can be defined as endowing (*en*) "the life force" (*prana*) into something, such as a thought, an idea, or even a thing or an individual. Quite literally, it means "blowing the breath of life."

"Kingdom of Heaven"

"The father's kingdom is spread out upon the earth / and people do not see it" is from *The Gnostic Gospels*, edited by Willis Barnstone and Marvin Meyer, page 69 (Boston: New Seeds Books/Shambhala, 2003).

"Wabi and Sabi"

The Japanese aesthetic of *sabi* celebrates that which is old and faded.

Northwest Park is in historic Windsor, Connecticut, and near Bradley International Airport. The park, a rural oasis surrounded by urban sprawl, is a 473-acre multirecreational facility operated by the town of Windsor, and offering an interpretive nature center, twelve miles of trails, and, in season, maple sugaring.